v. to float; to hope. To cause to float, to launch; to right a canoe; to listen with attention; to cheer up; to infuse life or hope into; to encourage; to be light; to float upon, as upon water. To insist upon; to persist; to offer, as a sacrifice. A buoyant force, as in the upward force of a fluid.

Ho'olana is dedicated to uplifting and supporting Hawai'i's many talented poets, writers, and artists, whose work we believe will inspire future generations.

Co-founders: Ryan Oishi, Tiare Picard, Sage U'ilani Takehiro

Visit our website at www.hoolanapublishing.org

ISBN: 979-8-9869167-1-2

Ho'olana Publishing says mahalo nui loa to Raymond and Dayle Oishi, Neil and Mia Oishi, and Jennifer Iseri for their generous support of this book.

Author's Acknowledgements

Mahalo nui loa to the amazing folks at Hoʻolana Publishing.
Ryan Oishi—Mahalo so much for your support, insights, and patience.
Sage Uʻilani Takehiro—I'm so thankful for your expertise and your *Honua*.
Tiare Picard—Mahalo for your energy and support.
I'm so blessed to have grown with such creative, kind, and spiritual folks.
Love you all.

Berton Hasebe—Mahalo nui loa for your generosity and mystical typeface.
Hyo Kwon—Mahalo nui loa for your expertise.

Kāwika Mahelona—Mahalo nui loa for the big work, the elegant work, your expertise.

My deepest gratitude to my Kumu Albert Wendt—Mahalo nui loa for your guidance.
I'm so blessed. My aloha to you, Reina, and Nia.
Professor Brandy Nālani McDougall—My literary sibling, I can't wait to give you a big hug,
you gorgeous you.
Kumu Dan Taulapapa McMullin—Mahalo nui loa for your magic.
Kumu Emelihter Kihleng—I love your poetry so much. Let's talk story again soon.
Professor Gary Pak—Mahalo nui loa for submitting my little story when I had just started at KCC.
Professor John David Zuern—You supported me all the way. Much love to you.
Kumu Kathy Banggo—Mahalo nui loa for your artistry and words of encouragement.
Kumu Patricia Grace—Mahalo nui loa for your guidance.
Kumu R. Zamora Linmark—Your work came into my life just when I needed it.
Professor Susan M. Schultz—Much love for years of encouragement and supporting other artists.
Kumu Wayne Marques—Mahalo nui loa for your care and teachings.
Kumu Witi Ihimaera—Mahalo nui loa for your storytelling and guidance.

Mahalo nui loa to the folks who imparted knowledge and offered support while I studied at the University of Hawaiʻi—Professor Ann Inoshita, Professor Ann Rayson, Professor Anne Kennedy, Professor Candace Fujikane, Professor Chip Hughes, Professor Cristina Bacchilega, Professor Cynthia Franklin, Professor David Baker, Ethel Watanabe, Professor Gail Harada, Professor Gaye Chan, Gayle Nagasako, Professor Glenn Man, Professor Haunani-Kay Trask, Dr. Jaimie Gusman Nagle, Professor Jim Henry, Joan Kaʻalekahi, Professor Joan Peters, Professor John Rieder, Professor Jonathan Morse, Kumu Joy Lehuanani Enomoto, Professor Judith Kellogg, Professor Kim Compoc, Professor Kimo Armitage, Professor Kristin McAndrews, Professor kuʻualoha hoʻomanawanui, Professor Laura E. Lyons, Professor Nandita Sharma, Professor Paul Lyons, Professor Peter H. Hoffenberg, Professor Pierre Asselin, Professor Robert Onopa, Professor Robert Sullivan, Professor Ruth Y. Hsu, Professor Ryan Omizo, Professor Sarah Allen, Professor Stephen Canham, Professor Suzanne Kosanke.

Mahalo nui loa and much love to the Maitland ʻohana.

Me ke aloha pumehana—Àngela Winbush, Bette Midler, Bootsy Collins, Chaka Khan, Cyndi Lauper, Dolly Parton, Epeli Hauʻofa, Gabby Pahinui, George Clinton, George Michael, George Takei, Gladys Knight, Grace Jones, Herb Kawainui Kāne, Imaikalani Kalahele, Izora Rhodes-Armstead, James Beard, James Ivory, Jeanie Tracy, Jennifer Saunders, Jessie Ware, John Waters, Joy Harjo, Kapono Beamer, Kate Bush, Keola Beamer, Kylie Minogue, Lena Kaulumau Waiʻaleʻale Machado, Lily Tomlin, Lois-Ann Yamanaka, Lolita de la Colina, Lupita D'Alessio, Luther Vandross, Madhur Jaffrey, Mariah Carey, Martha Wash, Meli'sa Morgan, Millie Jackson, Nichelle Nichols, Nickolas Ashford & Valerie Simpson, Nona Hendryx, Olivia Newton-John, P-Funk, Patti LaBelle, Paul Verhoeven, Pedro Almodóvar, Prince, Roger & Chaz Ebert, Sarah Dash, Sia Figiel, Stephanie Mills, Sylvester, Tawatha Agee, Teena Marie, Tusiata Avia, Whoopi Goldberg.

Aloha to my family—Kasey, my parents, Pua, JB, Kanaiʻa, Kaʻeo, Kekoa, Ryan, Krista, Ginger, Cooper, Autumn, Piko, Keola, Rainbow, Auntie Patti dem.

Ulu is dedicated to my kāne Kasey. You make every day fun, every night exciting.

Introduction by Brandy Nālani McDougall

Hōnaunau is a wahi pana, a richly storied place of great mana, sacredness, and sanctuary.

The ahupuaʻa of Hōnaunau extends from the verdant slopes of Mauna Loa to the calm and abundant Hōnaunau Bay. An ʻāina momona, or fertile land, of the moku of Kona, Hōnaunau's waters (kai, wai and muliwai) have renowned for their abundance of fish, shellfish and limu, while its uplands were full of ʻōhiʻa and koa trees for building and easily supported loʻi kalo, maiʻa, ʻuala, kō, and ʻulu. Hōnaunau has fed its kamaʻāina well for centuries, perhaps leading to its name, which means "to bite or chew."

Today, Hōnaunau is most known for its puʻuhonua, its "City of Refuge," which is now part of a park of 420 acres managed by the National Park Service. Along with the puʻuhonua, the park includes the royal palace grounds of the Keawe aliʻi and their fishponds, the Hale o Keawe, a Hale o Papa, or women's temple, the ʻĀleʻaleʻa Heiau, a Hale o Lono, ancient trails and roads, canoe landings, luakini burial caves, the Keoua and Kaʻahumanu stones, petroglyphs, and a spring. Thousands of tourists as well as several schools visit the Puʻuhonua o Hōnaunau every year.

Still, the park fails to capture much of the true history of Hōnaunau. These silences—of its kupaʻāina, its kamaʻāina, who have been the eyes of the land, waterways, and ocean for centuries, of its animals and plants, the voices of the ʻāina—have been only visceral until Kai Gaspar's magisterial and hauntingly beautiful poetry collection, *Ulu*.

A kupaʻāina of Hōnaunau, Kai Gaspar is a dear friend of mine, one with whom laughter comes easy. I first met him when we were both graduate students, taking creative writing courses at UH Mānoa. Aside from our both having the phenomenal Albert Wendt as our kumu (we often joke that this makes us literary siblings), we have also had a similar upbringing with our being raised on and by rural ʻāina on "neighbor" islands (as all other islands of the paeʻāina are known to the Oʻahu-centric). I write that we were raised *on* and *by* these ʻāina, because you can't live in ʻāina like Hōnaunau, Hawaiʻi or Kula, Maui without being outside on the ʻāina, without seeing the mana of the ʻāina around you in the rain, in the plants and animals, in the mists and fog. And you can't live in these ʻāina without it shaping who you are, without it teaching you how you should be in the world, raising you like kūpuna.

While neither of us were unaccustomed to urban living, sitting in the sterile, overly air-conditioned tundra of Kuykendall Hall classrooms of UH Mānoa in Honolulu seemed so different from our homes.

There were many times that I was thankful that Kai Gaspar was there, too, writing of Hōnaunau, warming and darkening (you learn to live with and love the dark in our ʻāina, too) the room with his stories.

As a poet, I have been inspired and influenced by much of his work, which is why it is such an honor to introduce Kai Gaspar and his first collection of poetry, *Ulu*. According to Mary Kawena Pukui and Samuel Elbert's *Hawaiian Dictionary*, ulu may be translated as "to grow, increase, spread;" "the increase or rising of the wind;" "to protect;" as well as "to be possessed by a god [or] inspired by a spirit, god, ideal, person, as for artistic creation;" as well as a "grove; assemblage, collection, or flock." Because our kūpuna also enjoyed the flexibility of ʻōlelo without modern diacriticals, we can also include the translation (and Hawaiian poeticisms) of ʻulu, as "breadfruit." According to one moʻolelo, the ʻulu tree grew from Kū's sacrifice and ensured, through the ʻulu's abundance that the people would never again know famine. Poetically and in keeping with the image of abundance form Kū, ʻulu may also refer to male genitalia in some traditions. Pukui notes that the ʻōlelo noʻeau "Kū ka ule, heʻe ka laho" or "The penis stands, the scrotum sags" is an expression that is "not meant to be vulgar," but to describe how "when the ule or pōule (breadfruit blossom) appears, it is the sign of the fruiting season. The young breadfruit first appears upright, and as the fruit grows larger, its stem bends so that it hangs downward" (*ʻŌlelo Noeʻau* 204).

At once, *Ulu* embodies and invokes all of these meanings—of sexuality, of growth and abundance, of protection, of possession, of hunger and satiety—through its storytelling rich in imagery and kaona (veiled cultural meaning).

A deft imagist, Gaspar immerses you in the raw surreality of an ʻāina that is at once ancestral and familiar, where the supernatural is natural and darkness provides safety, creating spaces for one to hide oneself or bury secrets. *Ulu* will lead you through a Hōnaunau that is both of and beyond the human, where sacrifices, large and small, consecrate the ulu, the spreading growth and abundance, of the ʻāina and moana, where refuge is found and lost and grown under (and depending on) the phases of the moon. Silver fireballs streak across the sky to find their victims, moʻo bark and summon, and weke weave through the waves to conjure ghosts, as the police raid the houses of the village. Gaspar's Hōnaunau is peopled, animaled, planted, and otherwise earthed with a multitude of personae who ulu, who grow and spread in ways both destructive and creative, who seed and feed and breed in the dark.

Ulu reveals Hōnaunau as a village alive, yet haunted and in perpetual transition and struggle. An ancestral moʻolelo of Hōnaunau recorded by Abraham Fornander tells of how a ʻulu tree sprung from Kāne there, but how "its fruits have been bitter or sour from that day to this" (268).

In keeping true to both this moʻolelo and to the name Hōnaunau, Gaspar shows the villagers, both human and non-human, are bitter and sour, bitten and chewed, even as they may bare their own teeth: a mother selling drugs to survive and using her knowledge of lāʻau to protect and heal; Claudia, Cora, and little brother, children survivors of sexual abuse; unicorn-loving Tamsen and Thaddeus, who is the narrator's first man he sees naked; Kuʻu Babe and Jin, a couple who procure whatever people need, the thieving Big Matt, wild Aunties and homophobic Uncles hiding from the cops, the devout Tūtū Clara, who prays to Ke Akua and sees the past and the future, a philandering father who is mostly gone, and the boy, the storyteller behind every poem, who is raised on all of their stories and creates more stories to protect himself and his loved ones. Like Hōnaunau, the boy bears witness to it all—offering healing moons and medicines—yet moves through the stories of the village like the Kēhau breeze of Kona.

Another ʻōlelo noʻeau, He aliʻi ka ʻāina, he kanaka ke kauwā, or The land is an aliʻi, humankind, only its servants, remains true throughout the collection. The ʻāina, Papahānaumoku, may feed herself even as she generously feeds others, and she may punish just as she may protect. Through her grace and power, we may hide, bury ourselves and our secrets, find nourishment, and live respectfully with others born from the earth, ocean, and sky. It is through her that we find the continuity and sanctuary to sustain us. As nā pua a Hawai'i, nā mamo a Hāloa, Gaspar reminds us, as Kanaka 'Ōiwi, to remember our genealogical ties to her, especially as we hunger.

So Hōnaunau lives and thrives as a wahi pana, as an old and newly storied place, as Gaspar honors, recollects, and chronicles both the troubled and the healing mo'olelo of his 'āina. You will not find this Hōnaunau on a map, nor in a tourist brochure. You must be guided by a kupa'āina over the old roads, across the cliffs, and through the forest. You must allow yourself to be bitten and swallowed by Hōnaunau's dark and mythic depths and heights, and keep your skull soft as a baby's so you may be fed and shaped by these poems.

Ho'omaika'i e Kai ē no kēia mau mo'olelo ulu no kou 'āina hānau aloha o Hōnaunau.

Contents

Hīnano

Supreme Vehicles 4

Big Sisters and Little Brother 5

Dirty Malo 18

Pūʻolo 20

Rock Bottom 25

Kūlolo 31

Budbud 33

Kawehi 40

Rubbish Dog Runs 42

Rubbish Dog Leaps 44

Tools for the Knee 46

ʻAlamihi

Mojo 50

Kahananui 57

Huacatay 61

Sure Save 63

Sea Goat 68

Bath/Shower 70

Alicorn 72

Koa 86

Bitters 88

Pua Kalikimaka 89

ʻUlu

Ānuenue 98

Kiawe 100

Kahuna Man 104

Buss Up Shut 107

Kulu 110

Make Man Sleep 118

Robby 122

Pō 131

Kukui 134

Pipipi 136

Ulu to grow as a child, ulu to rise in the wind, with the tide kai ulu, with the sun ka lā
Ulu to be possessed by a god, by a spirit, by a person, creation
Ulu, also unu, enter us, e ulu kini
Ulu the grove, of stars ulu hōkū, of birds ulu manu, of ships ulu moku, wa'a
Ulu the center of a net, and of a wa'a
By the center and the collection, enter us Kai māhū, with your māhū poems, word by word,
with your healing māhū, with your pain keiki māhū, with all the pain of your ulu,
all the glory of your ulu, all the savage grace of your ulu, the flowers and filth of your ulu,
the laws broken and the laws made of your ulu māhū, enter us and sing māhū, ka ulu māhū,
ho'oulu mai.

—Dan Taulapapa McMullin

Ulu

Hinano

Supreme Vehicles

Malibu uli speed-shifts in narrow Keoneʻele
Flaming tails whip my trifold's kukui stain
This dream urinates on black mud kapa

Ke hiki nei

I will plant night blooming ipu and observe the sun's withering habits
Pōpoki of lustrous dark suffered motorweight for my animal soul
May I bathe in compassionate oil and mourn in shelters of ease

Enemies hurl the engine down
Wound tread for Kealakekua blowout

O this night drive yearns
O the Mauna Loa's witness
O pōpoki's soul exits on route

Big Sisters and Little Brother

Big sister Claudia came during a strong sea.
After her mother's passing, her father made Claudia sleep in his bed and stole the money
she earned cooking in Kailua.
I gave her the trouble dolls who didn't know I pissed my sleep.
She taught me sugar, shoyu, and chunk light fry.

I tempted Kaipo from his guava lounge with birdseeds on my tongue, then swept before sunset
to keep the house lucky.
I swept before Mamu finished her pōpoki work leaving centipedes at the King's coil.
My mother thought Mamu hated brooms because she once knew them as tools of harm.
I warned Claudia about parking lot strangers who didn't know 'Mamu' was the code word.

The night without salt lines at doors, Claudia stabbed a centipede in our room, then pitched it
over buffalo grass.
We slept legs to sea.

In the morning, I found Kaipo's mangled skin near the Singer's pedal.
Mamu slept well under a matchstick pagoda.

Claudia and I wore towel crowns while suncatchers made complex displays and sandalwood smoke
rolled like waves at Keʻei.
We steamed our faces over boiling laxatives, then shared almonds from a kamani bowl
buffed with fat.

At the puʻuhonua, I led Claudia across the reef where Kupuna kāne-of-the-restorative-lā
found Kupuna wahine-of-repaired-nets.
They shared long life and a silver-haired kuleana to care for boys whose blood parents
left them on the shore.
Boys whose acne my mother treated with pānini ʻawaʻawa.
A boy called Blimp requested skin treatments in secret.

I showed Claudia the exposed Safety Rock.
Ocean dwellers rest on Safety Rock when thunderheads become sharp.

They smell like whale's breath, their skins may be covered in clusters of pīʻoe.
Sometimes after hurricanes, villagers find their teeth.

Our minds saw the sheltered bay where Tūtū Clara boarded the Hōkūleʻa, became guardian
of the voyage, then passed in Hilo.
My father rode the Hōkūleʻa and sent a letter from where the sun is cruel.

    Babe, how have you been?
    Hope everythings fine with you.
    What's been happening?
    How's everybody doing back there?

    I had a really exciting trip.
    It was a lot of fun and a lot of things happened.
    We had a really nice time.
    When we left the wind was nice and strong.
    It was a really spacey night.

When we hit the channel it was really heavy.
The moon was out all the time we were sailing and it was really beautiful.
There were some really big swells in the channel.
After a while we started catching the swell and surfed them.
Everybody were yelling and screaming having a good time.
All of a sudden one of the sails whipped over and snapped.
We broke our gaff and the boom.
Those are the two pieces holding the sails.
It broke into four pieces.
One of the pieces fell and hit Kimo in the head.
He passed out and was hanging over the side of the boat.
Roger ran over there and grabbed him just in time.

We had to take the sail apart and throw up the storm sails, which is really small.
During all that a 12 foot shark was swimming around the back.
It's a good sign of protection.
It took us eight hours to reach Maui.
Everybody was really stoked.

There was a change of plans because of the broken sail and a few other things.
Right now we're making repairs, so we've been really working hard.
We should be sailing to Moloka'i this weekend.

I'm running out of things to say.
I'll close for now, but I miss you very much, I miss Kona, and I love you.
Take good care of yourself and God bless you.
Lots of Love + Aloha

Claudia and I maneuvered the papamū's pebbles until our budbud was gone.
When I lived in Tūtū Clara's shack, the budbud lady would hūi! with a foil-lined soda box
full of budbud.
The indulgence made me 'ami in a temporary malo I started by sticking tissue between my cheeks.

My budbud jones assumed the pu'uhonua hale with the choicest paint job was our source
of coconut alchemy.
I never spocked anyone enter or leave, only an empty soda box, mice trapping themselves
in ripe papayas, mongoose enjoying mutual grooming.
Sometimes the budbud lady appeared as far south as Ka'ū.

A visitor with my father's scowl appeared at the shack but didn't hūi! from the road.
My father told my mother stay home while he met the visitor who mirrored
his ʻehu and complexion.
My mother followed them to the heiau where they peered across the bay until companion kiʻi
of waterfinders saw my father cry.

He shot mongoose through floorboards and let the stench anger my mother.
After she smelled deception on his ule, he ran to the puʻuhonua and wove frond mats for sleeping.
My mother found him fooling with a haole from Kailua.
She was being stink my mother said.
She was stink.
My mother passed me to the women of the launch wall before she wound the town woman's
ponytail around her hand and beat her.
Then my father broke my mother's jaw.

Aunties called hūi! from the gourd yard and presented their handsome sons.
My mother saved face as aunties tried luring her up the coffeeland where naio makika mesmerize
in rusted rain barrels.

She hid a photo of herself and an uncle from Josephine who raped her when she could still predict
visitors and telephone calls.
He told her it's all a dream, but she knew it wasn't.
After his concern for a posh monument rotted, my mother said 'I'm glad he's dead.'
Claudia and I enjoyed warm lau niu singing where my mother's elbows flared for the camera.
We ate our snared 'a'ama from a bucket that smelled of intertides and Saloon Pilot.

While seeking the sunset pleasure of rotting noni, Claudia chose to stay as big sister.
We watched the versina flash.
We talked with auntie who was so devout in her kino kanaka, a bloodstained cross
marked her kino manō's head.

Claudia was last seen near Keāhole.
When my mother dropped her at work, Claudia kept saying come check the schedule.
My mother didn't know they were being watched.
Claudia left a Pee-Chee of equations centered on the page.
We left her a coral message near Keāhole on the 'a'ā between love letters and prayers.
We turned a broken teeth smile into a message north of Keāhole.

My second big sister Cora shed blonde hair, easy to spock for 'anā'anā.
We pulled the backdoor's security spike so her coffeeland boy could enter after dark and whisper
'now I know you're mine.'
I watched them dream in the banana grove's erratic shadows.
My mother showed Cora sensible places for machete in a house.

Before little brother was to come, my mother told me his father stuck a broom handle inside him.
Little brother had trouble speaking and holding a ball.

Melvin was reporting on Momotarō's weaponry when Mrs. Arai saw one 'uku jump.
She told the class how shameful for Melvin to bring his filth from home.
I saw him descend the hill where haole kids repaired shoes and broken windows with duct tape.
While Mrs. Arai called us stupid for not marching to Pretoria in unison, I was wearing inside out
my mother's shirt that stuck finger and read 'Hey Russia, Shoot This Bird Down.'

After Mrs. Ikeda said kids who misspelled 'John' were stupid, I lit her face
with sunlight reflected from my koa hand mirror.

She demanded I stop gathering ti leaves, then said she would no longer call me Kai
because it wasn't my 'legal name.'
She asked my mother why I pursued girl company, why I painted a self-portrait called
Queen of the Flaming Knife.
My mother said I didn't waste time around boys who talk pilau and if she wanted to 'get legal,'
she better say Kāhea O Ke Kai O Kalani every time.

Mrs. Ikeda made me explain my girl company for an impromptu tell.

    Rani mahalos when I give her my oven's macaroons in tinsel covered dioramas.
    She doesn't call me faggot.

    Gertrude curls fingers into hooves, gallops on asphalt, nickers from the gut 'I'm here.'
    She gave me a rocking horse advent with gold foil candy and some doors removed.
    Horses don't say faggot.

    Jessica will say she's making doodoo, but don't mind because it's important I take her Hilo
    soon to escape lagoon-watching heron.

I'll bend knees in the dirty moku where hungry mechanics not easily tired
crave an exchange.

Jessica and I will sample iris bergamot perfumes before I drop her Prince Kūhiō Plaza
so wā uʻi she and her ipo of furrowed physique can press heads under a movie poster
that wants to know How many times can you die for love?
Jessica doesn't call me faggot.

I pinned boiled ti leaves for little brother's lei under my big toe and twisted.
Who from Kealakekua could put a broom handle inside little brother?

During a raffle of unwanted property, Mrs. Ikeda said I held the big box's lucky number.
She announced I won Miss America when I saw fading roses.
Kids asked what can be done with such a worthless box?
I sun-dried the petals for display, even the ones my mother called jealous yellow.

Some kids couldn't offer at the June lūʻau, so Mrs. Arai and Mrs. Ikeda had them sit in a corner
to watch others eat.

Aunties from CPS said little brother joined a more prepared 'ohana.
I draped his ti leaf lei over blown up photos of the pu'uhonua.

Kupuna Place taught us the 'ili'ili clack.
We gathered ali'ipoe for Kupuna Mahi's gourd rattle dance.
Kūpuna smiled big to call us a-k-a-m-a-i.
Kupuna Mahi spoke of amorous kāne who seduced with nose flutes.
Kupuna Place explained how the queen's bidet cleaned her all up.
When kūpuna strummed for 'E hau'oli e nā 'ōpio o Hawai'i nei 'Oli ē! 'Oli ē!'
my call was to little brother.

Dirty Malo

A rum woman of Kona cured pig maladies
and handled corrupt eras with her battle pike

She cruised Ka'ū's steady 'a'ali'i
Her vis-à-vis impulse lifted skilled warriors
in the pua 'ula of low spreading forms

The multitude honored guardian stars
then vanished devils on Ka Lae's twist

While weke wove phantasms below the mouse-skin shrine
expert hawk prayed kee-oh!
for those spitting second growth ʻuala into offspring

A woman of desirous Kona, there in Kaʻū
made bait sticks from ancient ʻaʻaliʻi who endure wildfires
and return in mottled combinations

Pūʻolo

When I saw the silver-tailed akua lele streak toward Keauhou, we had just moved south
after the police raid.
My mother tightened her red sarong knot and said must be a Hoʻokena conjurer.
She removed her panties, then descended the hill with machete.

Tamsen motioned from her houselight.
She had never seen the akua lele.
An auntie destroyed one over Hōnaunau by throwing her urine skyward.
I stabbed like the sharp-tailed kala to make it explode.

Say kūkae pilau.
Tamsen said it.
Kūkae pilau.
The stink rises.
Kūkae pilau.
The stink is upright.

We chanted on a terrace of true ʻawapuhi.
Eat my shit.
The stink rises.
Eat my shit.
Kūkae pilau.

I made my body a holy cross the way Tūtū Clara greeted dawn.
Ke Akua, send the akua lele back to its keeper.

Tamsen handed me a blunted alicorn from her display.
A mountain vapor gave me gooseflesh, she said don't look back, Thaddeus is naked.

I looked back.
Thaddeus was there, posed like the devil tarot's chained man.
I saw his thick loli, his curled hulu.
I had visions in the time it takes for the sweetest hua ʻai to fall and hit ground.
The transformer blasted sparks through a grove of true banana.
Since lights fell and the moon was braided, I ran from my first natural kāne without being seen.

The akua lele was gone.

My mother ascended the path I lined with reflective ragwort and comfrey good for poultices.
She washed urine from her hands and lit lamps for us to hang ti leaves in high corners.
She reminded—kūkae pilau, don't be shame, I love you all the way to Ke Akua's house.
I watched my reflection untie my hair.

Thaddeus swam naked while floating rum bottles at Keoneʻele.
Tamsen 'recharged' quartz in the puʻuhonua and let her dog Scream Queen shit in the hibiscus
garden my mother tended.
During a moon that favors disguises, my mother shared Almadén and sold them coke.
Tamsen let me indulge on Thaddeus's leathery bed smell.
I studied the unicorns she promised would be mine someday, but I knew her feelings
were temporary.
She explained how the desperate ones killed themselves, then stirred our wine with an alicorn
to counteract poison.

My mother placed the big jade she carried from Hōnaunau under the door crescent.
Thaddeus's Tuxedo-the-dapper-cat enjoyed pissing on the jade who was older than me,
so my mother said she was 'going Viet Cong' and fashioned a bamboo abatis.
After Tuxedo blinded my pōpoki Bow, I rubbed his wounds with young kukui juice.
Tuxedo pissed until the big jade died, so my mother killed him with an arrow.

I licked honeysuckle tails and saw three traveling lights flicker up Mauna Loa.
I dreamed barefoot boys chasing over salt wells, squeezing loli, shooting white threads.
They pissed on each other's man o' war stings for relief.
They swallowed hala pulp and chanted 'let da muthafucka burn!'

Waves rolled a little girl's shit until her brother buried it beyond high tide.
He told her 'don't chant like boys, say fatabula burn.'
But she continued 'muthafucka.'

A boy with ʻukiʻuki eyes climbed from a sea he calmed into a mirrored state.
I couldn't see myself reflected in his gaze, only slow clouds meeting.
He shared mountain water and showed me ukidama the colors of fresh līpahapaha.
He could tell what each had seen across limitless sea by pressing thumb to piko.

While dusk aroused hopes in ghost bats emerging from dead lau hala skirts, I offered to gather
ʻauhuhu for lagoon fishing if the boy made the poison.
I followed hungry pinao on the goat pen trail.
I followed strong hīnano toward the precipice where I saw tentacles in dens, tentacles thrusting,
tentacles at pearly mouths.

I collected ʻehu of hardwood males and stashed my bag for love work.
The boy's distant gourd whistle thanked ʻauhuhu feathers good before the passing of six nights.

I woke from burial caves and infant bones, I treated my face with first urine.
Village women said whoever cleans the toilet will have skin that reflects like the moon.

Rock Bottom

Tūtū Clara demanded my mother step her pregnant weight over tūtū's body.
Tūtū laughed after my mother said please don't return in a scary kino lau.
The Hilo people who removed us found so many scorpions in the shack, it writhed in lamplight.
A rainbow with plenty red appeared as we hauled tūtū's water tank past the Painted Church.

My mother's 'ōhi'a 'ai cravings while pregnant left a sweet stain on my leg.
Lucky we were living in the shelter and awe of Rock Bottom—get plenty 'ōhi'a 'ai.
My mother and Banza dug a lua where impatiens burst around our stink
to make undergrowth parapara.
I inhaled the lua's glistening dark from a deep lean.

While swinging sickle, my mother felt a tug, then found her severed acrylics spread across the dirt
in a favorable pattern.
She thanked her glamour tita for the acrylic experiment and Ke Akua for all ten fingers.

Banza sucked blunt smoke under nests I constructed from hen's eyes.
I self-induced mesmerism by watching the road blur through the Volkswagen hatch my mother
constructed for dropping evidence.

After I moved my cot into Hua's light, my spirit left through tear ducts
to wander the ghost mountain.
I ate rotten 'ulu and rubbed my tusks in the stamens of heavy bearers
whose bark decoctions treat thrush.
My mother massaged my spirit back into me.
She said I was grinding fruit too hard and biting sideways.

Through Akua, I purified my muddy bulk in streams.
A nectar loving 'apapane lifted my prayers for a sacrificed man I found on lau kī pekepeke,
my prayers for twin cousins born so small they fit into a shoebox.
I woke with a cut tongue and miscellaneous aches.

Banza insisted I shit in a plastic toilet he set under a mango tree, but the toilet couldn't hide hair
anyone might steal for ʻanāʻanā.
When the doctor's fingernail cut me inside, I visualized broken rice.

I called Auntie Eleanor's flame Uncle Jack because he was moustache-handsome
like a playing card.
He burned photos of auntie's kids and drowned the piece he used to separate some Kailua boys
from their supply.

ʻApapane imparted knowledge of ʻōhiʻa ʻai leaves tinged ʻula, so I touched my reddish birthmark,
then dipped my finger in auntie's beer when she wasn't looking.

My mother said slick boys cruise toilets—piss at the allamanda where everyone can see.
The toilet for kāne at Caps launderette revealed ink vulvas with chisel tip hairs
I thought carried signals like telephone cords.
I loitered with ketchup packets for vandalizing my stall and prayed any artist would return.

My hot salt made nice to a boy who shared coins the launderette spat.
Vented heat swirled between backbones of the place and a long stone wall
like the ones that fortified cities.
We schemed with oily fingers, then walked the dead corridor to learn what's at the end.

During a dream thirst, I found Uncle Jack's gnawed piko in a secondhand vanity
smeared with rat grease.

Kūlolo

Kuʻu Babe's fleshy red inspires a triple share while Jin asks Inés about occasional kāne.
She sent one home after he maimed her late summer profusion.
But he excites like Tito Rodríguez, so he'll return to love guzmania's smooth margins
and ylang ylang that enhances memory.
Kuʻu Babe pleases Inés of twelve siblings by finding her tree's elusive name.
Her mother said you will know a child's blue-black depths if you raise only one.

Kuʻu Babe swigs daiquiri and observes a girl dressed in morning dust troubleshoot her engine.
His torn cloves alleviate Jin's itch.
Jin finishes the flask while a tūtū inspects her silver roots with a hubcap, pisses in a dracaena grove
before zenaidas escort her home.

Kuʻu Babe makes kūlolo for the old city's Black Widow whose à la mode
elevated metropolitan drag.
Sometimes her husbands perished, and disciples find themselves kicked over the sea.

She granted Kuʻu Babe and Jin audience, but when they stayed ready with Veuve and adoration, she sent regret—fatigued from a whimsical malady.

Kūlolo for Shashi of the silver bob who the barkeep says smells like the blue slag cats
she made her kuleana.
While Shashi and Jin suck spirits through each other's straws, he accepts her invitation to eat hare on a Sunday.
Kūlolo for mother and daughter drinking pau hana rum where can.

Jin asks Inés if she still siphons her gas at dusk, if rubbing afflicted tongues
with the rompe banana's water was familiar.

Kuʻu Babe prepares canapés for noon cava, but Inés bought a fancy candelabra tall as harvest kō from a street dealer who backpacks a refrigerator door stocked with coffee, liquor, and bandages. A best tita recognized the candelabra from a looted tomb, so the day will be spent returning it before ghosts execute a search.

Budbud

Auntie Casey pool hustled men before losing teeth during heroin days.
Sweeping country clubs in her custody was better than boys shouting māhū!
outside my crown flower sanctuary.
When her dentures soaked on the commode, I pissed in the dark so I wouldn't ponder bad omens
and auntie's empty mouth.

Auntie soaped toilets flecked with shit.
She spoke of sawtooth haoles who kill understories and block water wherever they spread.
I rummaged unopened cans, then climbed lucky nuts to watch hirsute players stroke
near a heiau for potency.

Under a pastel of myself as a moustached man I wrote three fortunes.

> You will trade lei at Nāpoʻopoʻo for money, uhu, and true stories
> about Hōnaunau's springboard.

The trembling ʻōmaʻo in her upperstory will spock you searching crotches
on Puna's red plains.
She might ask in her slurred ʻōlelo—will the ʻawa nourish your mother
when she becomes a woman of the pit?

Déjà vu and limu supreme that looks like dog hair will please your ipo.
You will let tuberose wilt under a shared bed.

Auntie was mad when I shit so hard her toilet wouldn't flush.
My mother parked where Oshima's fluorescent buzz interrupted my prayer for a quiet mind.
Auntie wielded a new plunger like a weapon and showed me the price.
After my mother took her aside for a story tell, auntie hid the plunger backseat, then crouched
against my door to say don't worry about the money.

The poi had molded since my last return home.
My mother and I ate the poi with radishes and watched moths burn.
In a garden of climbing kupukupu, we sang ʻ ʻO Makalapua ulumāhiehie . . .ʼ

34

I kept a mourning dove called Mālie who made slow turns in mist.
My mother said Mālie's coo OO oo oo oo was the message 'bucks for lōlōs,' so middays we chanted
'bucks for lōlōs!'

Auntie Casey fed me papayas to help digestion and stitched me a Christmas stocking
from coffeeland burlap.
It smelled like a hundred pounds for a hundred bucks at the mill, like Uncle Dong's flatbed
floating me in monstera lavalava for parade.

My mother pranked auntie with show business schemes from an illustrious Ms. McGillicuddy.
Auntie earned a master's, went California for more CPS work, then met a sweet someone.
My mother could tell through infrequent telephone talk auntie was using again.

I cut green papayas while my mother signed her well-filled 'umeke with red nail polish.
We plucked Uncle Dong's malunggay, compared souring agents that made her 'ono
for pig's blood.

I splashed the blood-pumping spice that made kāne fiends.
I watched B-boys near Hale Hālāwai's toilet feel their mounded sources during preludes
and grip thighs as they spun.
The boss demanded pilau talk, but I offered budbud instead.
Sleepwalkers saw fish twitching on his kauila.

The boy with a burning midrib ate the tinolang manok I promised would make his body strong.
He had the twins of Ka'ūpūlehu tattooed on his calf, so when he danced they took turns
above and below.
His piko made me wonder what I would see if I stuck my thumb inside.

We walked the salty drag, past spocking kāne who could be coaxed from their stone wall
into buying liquor for an exchange.
One kāne remembered my spice and asked what I knew about Tonga.
I said there is coconut cream octopus, there are medicinal taproots seeking pō.
A sybil with dramatic lashes lit my iris on the boardwalk to say my na'au needed a backside dose.

Vermilion arcade lights flashed my brow while the boy won me a comb and the steady healing of rainbow jasper.
He fed a fat machine I never touched because elders said it was the devil's abode.
But the boy went all in for a long play of splitting kāne and making powerful downslurs.
His lips flushed pink like a marshland bloom when he signed his glory scores R-N-K.

He spit my wrist for the Tomoe Ame tattoo and said he was good at keeping the ink sharp.
An older brother of Kona Inn gifted us azure crystal cards for lucky rubbing.

The boy asked if the sybil made me shame.
He said she had kapakahi lashes and a smeared beauty mark.
I asked if he ever wore pajamas or pissed his sleep.
He said no, then told the truth.
I invited him up the mountain to pinball and share my first pajamas Auntie Casey said would make me a sophisticated kāne like Cary Grant.
I touched the reddish piko connecting his twins and said this is where your skin finished before you were born.

He climbed the plumeria most luscious in dark when the tinolang manok made our bodies strong.
We positioned the blooms, each inside the other until our lei was pau and our hands sticky.

An uncle stomped our partnership.
After he said plumeria made us too friendly, a pavilion pu'ukani sang Ei Nei
for lovers of the enduring style.

When I pissed the mattress, I was dreaming a mo'o lured me to Kona hospital's mortuary.
He showed me the severed leg of a man punished near the 'ulu lookout.
The leg was inside a KTA bag full of hungry 'alamihi.
The mo'o showed me a Ho'okena boy strangled on the road of the gods.
As I wiped blood from his nose, he opened his ulua eyes to call me.
The mo'o scooped them out because they're no good when cooked.
He tattooed my forehead and dragged me to where the sea is slippery.

I hid the wet sheet and whispered for my mother's remedies over the telephone.
Eat true aloe, but I couldn't find any.
Wrap a wet towel around my ule, but the towels weren't mine.
Auntie found the sheet and said not to bother my mother with in-house trouble.

I told auntie I would visit the gushing hill, smell the yellow excrement, then listen
to an 'io's counsel.
Auntie said yes, go and listen.

I told auntie I would gather pa'iniu as proof and weave the silver into a mat for day sleeping.
Auntie taught me the word envy.

Kawehi

Swing em, Auntie
Rhumba from your rancho lanai
Saucy, that's the way

I step left then push knees
Teasing right then pry open

Yes Auntie, strum down
the boa teases 'round
fluttering to your hot cha-cha

Gutter bird pecking tire grooves
howzit with you when Auntie honi honis
devotees who let their ribbons and frills go wherever they want

Ooh Auntie, those roselani plays you make from a Hawaiian moxie
capsizes experts, teaches newcomers to self-right
Wild dogs tell the story before it's over

Ear to pū, Auntie
do nose flute companions woo with their long breaths
do you hear cries of outcasts drowned at Kewalo

Rubbish Dog Runs

Dogs track the demigod stink ahead of weapon men
lighting their piss in the tungsten

While Big A puffs through her meerschaum
some men sing about a beauty who grips after the fitting and likes to ride
some mention night demons with slit genitals

The elusive pig dreams in brush piles, ruins nests of imperiled birds
The pig changes up MOs for more opportunistic eating

A gunslinger chokes the catch dog—rubbish kine, his head's not in it

While Big A restores with mahalo methods
some kāne become mālie like boys sharing breast milk
boys gathering 'uhaloa for emollients and better breathing

Mālie
until the demigod launches offense and the flora that eased dog's weaning spills on the gate

A gunslinger kicks his choleric temperament into the catch dog's naʻau
Big A curses the offender's testicles so his nights of hiki nō! are past

Big A's and her kāne's motives to get weak rouses a wind that tightens skinned pigs
Big A's motive to get worn strokes down on her kāne's delicate skin

Rubbish Dog Leaps

Rubbish dog
climbs disturbed terrain
to smell the enduring olonā

Rubbish dog
climbs the pali from moth dusk

She's past her days of strength
and floods tumble her down to road-sweet ginger
but she needs no calling

Rubbish dog
climbs the iron summit

As we exchange breath
on the precipice where there's no hiding
rubbish dog says look for her in shadows of pōhuehue
that stimulates birth and drives fish into nets

Rubbish dog
regards her shifting reflection
and undersea blooms in this wā of abundance

Go rubbish dog—leap!

But she needs no calling

Tools for the Knee

The fire-headed manō delivers tools for you

Pōhaku of destructive rains sink the lure
Shells cooked to night's luster for you

A fish of sour temperament is your food
Tūtū's spine of the red crevice is a tool for you

Noni juice and defiant fishes are your food
Kō of Muku dark sweetens bark tonic for you

Long ti to purify
The way is clear for you
Lūheʻe lures rot in the knee for you

Waves take your lei of spiny limu
The affliction is caught
The affliction is cut

A fighting fish for you
It is cut

‘Alamihi

Mojo

I squeezed 'awapuhi heads to collect the aromatic slime in bottles marked 'ninjin elixir' I dug from Rock Bottom.
I left the bottles on the lowest baño step for the coffeeland god after word spread she had 'ukus and burned her scalp with a towel soaked in kerosene.

When the god emerged from a sundown bathe, her towel crown smelled like engine.
I said the moa kāne crows too soon, he gives me mattress-pissing dreams about Mojo.
But coffeeland gods move fast and her steam made me swoon.

Mojo 'io-eyed the haole who tested film on kids.
Mojo never scolded boys for limp wrist.
Mojo could freeze Grandma Milla's carambola goat patrol until gathering was pau.
Mojo fancied mountain women.
Mojo crashed and died.

My mother said some aunties will claim bad brakes—honi Ke Akua.
Some uncles will claim slender moon—aloha Ke Akua.
So, mum's the word.

I asked my needle and thread did Mojo crash the stones?
The needle said yes.

Does she eat the yellow centipede when mountain people sleep?
The needle spun.

She doesn't hunt kids whistling in dark?
The needle was still.

I crouched in a sundry that sold erotic magazines between bright velour and postcard carousels.
Legendary people waved 'I'll be seeing you' to lovers who enjoyed slow retreats.
The active, salt-thickened pages swore secrets of the handsome-eyed kole.
I slipped the knowledge into my underwear, mature lowlands pressed my na'au.

On my way to the pig's coil, I saw kāne joining nets, kāne beating the water.
I wanted the kole raw, the darkest ones buried in my foundation.
I wanted sleep with crystallized ʻehu kai in my hair.

Banyan mynahs spocked me gathering—for what, the lauaʻe?
I savored my carambola, told them for what.
They laughed at my gathering bag and said coffeeland gods know common lauaʻe from the peʻahi
that perfumes choice kapa.

The mynahs threatened to shit on me if I didn't give tribute from my open hand.
But the tide would soon reveal shoals where leaping ʻaha frighten those in small boats.
How easy to wash the shit, then press my face against an ice shave's silver grill for more comfort.

The mynahs swooped some lauaʻe, so I gave coins and a button already loose.
The mynahs kept on—here is a district acquired by war, give the place your tears.

I laughed and said my ancestors who became pueo have been known to blot the sun and destroy
enemies with the fiercest shitting of a leeward parliament.
I spit at the snatchers of land, I spit at the supreme.

The mynahs sought the groundskeeping sorcerer, so I threatened to slit their tongues
and make them frequent mimics.
They would say 'good morning, drink coppee' like Uncle Marcelino's coffeeland pet.
Across the road, a shorthaired dog pissed on the burned coral of Moku'aikaua.

A kāne picked me up in a sandy hot hatch rimmed with masking tape.
His skin fluctuated mackerel patterns when he rubbed my scar.
I said my mother stuck lightning in my ear for strength, but I preferred a more steadfast energy.
He said he lived alone where nenue jump nets and can be hard to catch.
I asked how do you eat them?
He said raw is best, then asked the same.

When he touched my blood clot, his breath tasted spicy like limu lipoa.
I told him how HeShe the peach face went mad while perched on my thumb.

I buried HeShe's slaughtered cage mate under lemongrass so I could consume his memories.
During a night of upright energy, HeShe butchered a charm that tried hiding in a wicker cocoon.
I buried them under lemongrass and returned HeShe to the bird man who sent an angry letter
after HeShe slaughtered everyone in his grand cage.

The kāne described each face of a four-emotion glove puppet that followed him from kid time.
He never rethreaded its shame face and wanted a new one.
So, I gave him a face.

He said he could read minds because waves stirred his sleep.
I conjured the knowledge in my gathering bag for us to lock sight.
I saw him dreaming on heiau stones while 'ōhi'a posts burned.
He saw a performer with eyes like the kole—maybe I would enjoy seeing him wrestle brutes,
then gush.

When he invited my knowledge of Waipi'o, I said Tūtū Clara callused her shoulders
during her wā u'i packing kalo up slopes of luxuriant growth.
She thrashed a shark man who was eating villagers.

Some undersea passages require three days water in unbreachable vessels.
'O'opu rest in mud.

He parked at Kona Theater and asked if 'o'opu cooked in fragrant leaves was familiar—
his throat had become 'ono for it.
He let me humble myself on the warmth of his seat, then said boy, go home.

I pondered the projection booth that villagers warned was diseased because a transient
with Hep C slept there.
I tasted my carambola's sweet milu.
My fingers cooled in a rising wind until I wiped them on my sleeve.

I saw the coffeeland god scent her bra with laua'e before slipping into a headstrong kāne's
El Camino the color of yellowing ginger leaves.
They drove Onomea to do the donkey way.
Onomea for sunrise in the collapsed arch.

I hid Mojo's brush where tires didn't skid and watched coffee branches wave a hui hou.
I distracted chickens so they wouldn't see me bury the hair.

My mother tied rubbish bags around my feet for ascending Mauna Kea, then passed her boot flask.
A rumbling cousin known to eat sweets dropped in cinder opened a slope race challenge,
but none would risk outdoing her.
Before reaching Waiau of the eroded cone, I was overcome by giddiness and sleep.
I filled an alfalfa sprouting jar with tap water the coffeeland god poured at Mojo's crash.

My best tita and I worked the hoshidana slide to protect our harvest.
We shared stories about Mojo over the Hōnaunau brew and read the offgrade grounds left in cups.

Kahananui

When I found my mother poking needle on Mateo's futon, her eyes were 'ū'ū luminous.
She blamed her cocaine stammer on a brother who had stabbed her in the neck
with a sharpened tinker toy.
But this time she was singing about guns behind mirrors.
A policeman told me if there are guns, keep them away.
I said she was delirious, no need look.

Auntie Casey drove me from the jailhouse to her lanai's kalakoa sofa where I could see
Mateo's dark window.
Auntie Silvana emerged from night to tell me how her little brother packed burdens
that curved his spine.
Before he threw them into the maggot heaps at Ke'ei, auntie said his mind traveled backward,
and my mind would travel backward too if I didn't go Ke'ei.

My mother said her allure made Auntie Silvana jealous—that's why she tried forcing
ho'oponopono on O'ahu for six months,
that's why she put a hex on the tarot deck she gifted in 1980.
Some villagers said they would have comforted me, but my mother kept my whereabouts
and testimonies hidden.

During a onetime visit, my father introduced a military haole whose manicure
couldn't grip a cane knife.
She invited my mother for lines in the bridal hut just before vows, but my mother's entry
made the haole scream so loud the officiant's lips jutted like a gun muzzle.
She threatened to cancel a Tom Selleck lookalike if I told my father she swigged liquor
while hāpai.
The lookalike arrived drunk.
When I received my father's temporary address at Hālawa Correctional, she said the sting
was a frameup.
She taught me the word dyke.

I electrical taped a vinyl recliner for Grandma Virgie's rest after her ascent on the road of the gods
and 'eh, I watching da Equalizah' if anyone interrupted.
She said the fifty bucks I earned gathering macadamia covered my back-to-school Woolworth bill
that I later learned was double.
Poolhall carousers thought her son avoided some fleshly lust to narc.
My mother seduced him during our untroubled wā and found out.

Mateo worked Kohala freighters that brought glass frying pans and rent-to-own furniture.
We loaded metal-heavy boxes into his Fairmount, then hid them in a defunct water tank
shaded by sweet acacia.
He gave my mother the same orchid perfume he gave his daughter before she fled to Venezuela.
My mother said his daughter became like a wife, and if he ever touched me, I should tell.

In exchange for coke, a Kainaliu artist gave Mateo paintings of women kissing and salting fish,
women bathing and drinking 'awa.
Each canvas had been slashed X.
My mother said the artist had a jealous ipo who sold jewelries across Sandy's Drive In.

I spocked to know her passion eyes.
But instead, there were girls knotting shirts under their breasts.
Girls sticking tongues at erect zealots.
Titas sucking liliko'i and swatting bees around their lips.

I conspired with my reflection to orchestrate romance across the washerette.
I received pīkake for pinning up my hair, then rouged with the lipstick my mother used
to leave a message on Mateo's mirror.

> Now that the body is unclothed, so now is the face.
> Today, tomorrow, loving you.

Huacatay

A kahuna woman smelled Silvia's scalp—there is doodoo here.
Silvia opened a bodega her womanizing ex closed with money and connections.
She followed the kahuna's remedy by screaming his name into the jungle.

After Eddie Palmieri shakes the ancient sugarloaf, Sylvia drives Kuʻu Babe and Jin
to the marine corps base for dinner with Peruvians who met through a newsletter.
Silvia says rubbishing a key bump before crossing from Lima is always last minute.

While Vilma prepares papa a la huancaína and cau cau, guests heckle the television
when a dashing dilettante in business casual adds mangos to ceviche.
Vilma's alcove displays her husband's service medals and framed certificate of naturalization.

Jin admires a waʻa moored above 'Peru' in gold airbrush.
Vilma says 'That is the jungle. That is my home.'
Her dog, a walking ipu heke, shows Kuʻu Babe huacatay in their gloaming.

During a newsbreak about Titicaca, Silvia says the caca side is Bolivia's.

Vilma shares smuggled seeds and choreography she brought from her village.
After a chic neighbor in a geometric jumpsuit crashes to sip pisco and divulge romantic scandals,
Vilma's best tita whispers 'Sonia is drama. Don't go clubbing with her.'
But Jin continues fawning over Sonia's sculpted blush while Kuʻu Babe slips Sonia's phone number
into a safe place.

Silvia says papa seca is food for Kīnaʻu Street rendezvous.
Kuʻu Babe makes his carapulcra rich with bones in.

Sure Save

Augustine borrowed our VCR to enjoy his Gallagher tapes until my mother caught him peeping from the boneyard.
She laughed whenever Augustine telephoned for 'a dime bag of parsley.'
His wife June gave us tickets to a ventriloquist whose dummy made Augustine and my mother stage marriage and can-can.
She ended the dummy's gust, then warned me against trusting Gallagher fans—
their thinking ain't right.

While June labored for her second child, I guarded her first.
I crocheted a covering that became a pinching eel, corms of mana uliuli, a sea
where skin is bruised.

Before June's mother left the village, she recorded my work with a new ink ribbon.

    Shine wood, stain treat, rub mother's yes joint, rotate big toes, rub mother's beer parlor
    Casanova, don't pose like Jody Watley while frying corned beef, track food stamps,

buy tampons, pressed powder, sandalwood, sardines, 'Let the bearer of this note buy two
boxes Benson & Hedges Ultra Lights,' wipe lipstick kiss from mirror, clean toilet,
don't water garden with limp wrist, cook rice, cook hekka.

I once helped Snow White crack padlocks for some B&E in a story protected by an extensively
tested wipe-clean book cover, but the writer never mentioned food stamps.

Casanova gave my mother 'uku papa, then let me squeeze his na'au
during a quick holoholo motorcycle that scarred my leg.

The passage mouth to the toilet for kāne gaped under the royal flame's dripping puhi.
Urinals surged like Hiʻilawe nourishing stream life.
Upright pōule rubbed each other in winds that had slackened and reversed.
The gum spattered 'ulu made my tongue curl like lei palaoa.

I searched for boys to slacken in the passage, but my mother became suspicious, so I postponed
through her routine.
She was running a Section 8 scam with Auntie Charlene whose 'ohana wasn't in the village long.

My mother shared Dexedrine, coke, and laughs over auntie's redos from her former profession
dubbing pornographic films.
Auntie taught me the word prophylactic.

I postponed through my mother's routine.
She was sharing and dealing coke with Auntie Mildred whose 'ohana wasn't in the village long.
While receiving goods and writing my mother's Honduran sponsor daughter Delsis, they agreed
she was sending coded requests for cash only to bypass Christian Children's Fund.
Their shiny 'ōpelu eyes spocked musicians strumming The Twilight Zone theme
near the post office and thought they were cops until a bus arrived for adults with disabilities.

My mother found a trail of stolen weed from her drying space to auntie's door but forgave
after auntie helped my mother organize a gang thump on an ipo who beat breastfeeding women
and pointed guns in their faces.
He said my mother was orphaned because her mother cruised with strange men and deserved
a roadside death like a whore.
He destroyed Tūtū Clara's rosary, my baby footprints in ink, my autograph
from María Conchita Alonso.

When the moon lured beer parlor kāne, I scuttled through the passage like a yellow-backed ʻaʻama.
Hiʻilawe's mist freed the dedicated night queen.

A pole fishing kāne spit where kāhuna inserted glassy shafts that melted for laxative effects.
Anyone spread in joint action knew the guidance was deluxe.

Greenful kāne massaged hips while curved faucets sprayed for laxative effects.
Experts pounded the stupefying ʻākia roots, then grouped their tips to split any fighter.
I slid in cloudy waters that went over, blown by the heaven.

Kāhuna pounded the hairy ʻauhuhu good for ʻanāʻanā.
Anyone in unlocked stalls received the concoction to feel rip currents at Kamehame.

I struggled like a drowning man until defeated.
I dreamed I was daubed with excrement, which meant money was coming.

Sea Goat

I rub voiceless thighs while pō delivers my man
handsome like silver-streaked kukui

Moʻo tek tek tek on my breadfruit door and foresee
blessings that cling to firstborns
enjoying ʻoʻopu from gourds cut endlong

I spread lau maiʻa on my night-longing mattress to calm
intricate scale patterns transforming my back

ʻIo in her moderate v asks
how will your bone weight rise ʻehu style
if you pursue moʻo through blood burning dark

But I tek tek tek and hunt pōnalo
while my man heaves prayers into the exalted stratum

There him
stoking shadows for flight

There him
making firmament red

I thank the center post of our pili sweet
while my man thatches from the bottom frame up

He pleases his bundle with bone-close aku
He keeps coronas flaring

Gusts trouble the receding kee-oh! above bundle feeders
who the MC of phantoms and mating games decreed
an inseverable link

I mix rotted trunk and hau for a five-cycle medicine
that hastens a cleansing shit

Bath/Shower

(Off)

Oh fancy bath/shower
gleaming in this electric house

How many from the swelling darkness
have you confused with your flow controls

Don't shame me
I won't return like a begging fly

Oh fancy bath/shower
I smell of limu and wind fire
The luna makes this anus sputter

What kāne on the town will want such a worthless companion
I'm the pilipili caught in fur of upright animals

(On)

Oh bath/shower
your waters stab like wana
Am I unwelcome

You blast a Kona storm on my tin roof
Is your voice never soft

Bathwaters of Hōnaunau caress like the ʻilima
I let wilt around my neck

But mahalo bath/shower
I will cruise salty skindivers and draw kāne on the town
I'm no longer the unwashed fool

Alicorn

My mother returned from Paradise with a jeweled cane spider and a concern for how high
it should lift her black calf-length.
I said either hip since she was strong in both legs.

At the welfare inquiry that smelled like glue, a tita advised my mother to turn her diamond ring
upside down.
When Mrs. Fang of teardrop pearls asked who owned our Sakamoto electrics, we showed proof—
uncle owned the Sakamoto electrics.
A Miloli'i man blew snot onto the asphalt and shouted skyward—dey trying fo burn me!

I learned metric by cutting coke.
My mother said cut well, cut fair, don't let those cats think you're a jive muthafucka.

The Villanuevas erected a kapu on their gardenias, but I picked two choice ones and sprayed
the 'ukus while my mother peeled out.
Lola-of-the-road who perched above Dodo mortuary never looked toward my telepathy.

At Kainaliu's toilet for kāne, I smelled telephone numbers splashed with cake-water and piss.
I copied 328s that showed devotion in their upward curves.
If I dialed, kāne would blow through bone ridges hoehoe to make me a best companion.

In my mother's right-hand chronicle, I found 8s drawn like split elliptics, muscular upstrokes
of the line 'semi-horny, semi-religious.'
My mother's left-hand pressure for 'semi-horny, semi-religious' in another pocket chronicle
dug trenches that bled through next pages.

Her seafaring brother adored a Cebu City woman with poems I thought expressed
a hairy man's sensitivity.
But my mother spit and said more like she stuck a finger up his ass and now he's in love,
like her pussy lined with gold.
She prayed, then destroyed photos he sent of a diseased Oceanic man caught in softbox light.

During uncle's onetime visit, I spied him oiling his luminous hulu, legs to sea
on a trail of sweet stink lantana.
I rubbed myself with the lubricating pā'aila good for fever.

My mother said call cops if she didn't return from room 412 by sunset.
She gave me an alibi and twenty bucks in a peacock wicker lounge where I watched 'ā pele
eating trespassers, gardenia 'ukus crawling across my major arcana.
I called the two of cups Kai and Kawai after boys from an American Savings Bank promo
pressed on a 45.
They played four-handed string games, shared skillful tillage, implored gods of husbandmen
for the breakthrough above, the wetness below.

My mother felt clean when she saw kūkaelio in her colonic tube.
She said go, but I preferred castor oil in Exchange.

My father borrowed my mother's gold Bug and took me glass-bottom cruising along breaks
for Kona's longest rides.
Rhythmic kāne danced the hardness that knots within to make assets tight.
He parked up a flirt's Hōlualoa bungalow so fast it was like riding wet pili.
I hit the dashboard when he rammed a night-wandering cow who stumbled to the ʻulu lookout,
then fell into the pit.

My mother returned from Paradise with rubbish bags of weed and a bird-flower muʻumuʻu
I burned during fevered ironing.
I measured eighths and oh-zees, and sniffed pak fah yeow.
My mother recalled a Hilo brothel where The Malasada Queen tightened thumbscrews
on unruly johns.

At fire rescue, I hid between jaboticabas and filled my gathering bag.
I wore a skin like the lauʻīpala's so Lola-of-the-road might see.
While my mother collected from a glassmith tita, her son showed me his loʻi, his purple leaf scars.

I traced veins of the unforgettable champak.
I saddled the ass he called Valentine.
He gripped his ʻōʻō for leading me this way, that way, around his embankments.
We bathed in a pool he blushed ʻōhelo and stirred with sawing motions.

He said let's climb the pali for royal enjoyment, let's play on jutting rocks.
I promised to mount the highest if he showed me his strongest palm.
He had a passion mesh below his thumb and a tricky constellation.
When we held hands and jumped, we lit the sky like burning pāpala caught in updrafts.

During an 'Ole moon, my mother told me the boy was hit by a car.
His mother scattered him where he would generate forests and nēnē might feed on his kino.
My mother gave me the mottled goblet his mother created through her blowpipe.

Sometimes I hung 'ōhelo leaves for infusions I drank in the calm of Kona.
Sometimes I licked Pele's smoke from two fingers.

I wore the gold kihikihi Cain won my mother at Konawaena auction, prayed Lola-of-the-road
would see my shine.
I decorated Narcotics Anonymous with pink bougainvillea he cut from Hōnaunau.

A Kahaluʻu family found me outside St. Michael's reading auguries for the coming epoch.
The Kahaluʻu woman had me choose a path to Eclipse.
I chose the crescent shade so we could kick like steady mudhens, admire māhū in Shiseido
doing ʻami ʻōniu under traffic lights.
I prayed for long life in the residing māhū's dizzying fragrances.

The Kahaluʻu boy nursed a sickly bird that flew above the destroyed breakwater.
I told about Rainbow who appeared with tail feathers someone painted green.
Rainbow ate every day in my house while molting wing feathers someone painted red.
Rainbow balanced on coaxial cables with her rounded stumps.

Ka naiʻa glided from under the horizon to ask 'Miss Rainbow, pehea ʻoe?'
while she stretched above the muck.
During breeding seasons, I cleaned the dried excrement that made Rainbow limp.
Rainbow sheltered two wind-tumbled fledglings until the egg moon lit their strength.

When the pianist made Kui Lee's melody chirp from the instrument, the crooning Kahaluʻu man
promised to remember me.

I told the Kahaluʻu family that weekend revelers snorted coke in the toilets and stabbed each other
under the kamani's blunt tips.

I saved the shells of pūpū we ate.

My mother returned from Paradise to say the KS lesions were in Auntie Faye's lungs.
When auntie and her son Skyler came to the village, she couldn't work a stove, so my mother taught her adobo, cascaron, delicacies of the land.
'Opiuma shaded the sanctuary where auntie sang with Slack Sax.
My mother broke auntie's mout with chili con pickled pigs feet, kimchi, yellow peppers, chili water, and mayonnaise.
I reported on levitation while Skyler pressed my bedspread's alicorn.
Tūtū Clara once sent levitating winds after I fell headfirst stretching for bananas over 'a'ā.

Coffeeland kids ask what's in New York Skyler boy?
What's in da city?

Mom was in the city getting wise.
Some gentlemen friends were rough—she almost could not do it.

Pehea ʻoe Skyler boy?
How's da health?

I'm all pau bathe, but night sweats are new—I almost cannot sleep it.
Auntie-mommy sucked a bee stinger from my sole.

How's da village Skyler boy?
How's Hawaiʻi nei?

Poi makes my bones big.
I run barefoot, and Uncle Dong says the meat is black dog.

Good fo you Skyler boy.
You calm your ma's fever, and you are wise.
You eat mana ulu—your mind has seen Kona.

Auntie Faye reserved my place in the 'opiuma shade, close to the kahuna.
The kahuna levitated a spinning bundle that spread the fresh living smells of Hōnaunau.
The kahuna's voice hastened pomegranate stains on my lips, the silver points in her eyes blinded anyone who looked.

I dreamed the kahuna left chewed 'ulu within my reach.
Skyler and I needed the kahuna's guidance, but my mother said Chaka Khan
doesn't live in the 'opiuma.
I hung an image of Kahuna Khan over Skyler's bed so he could dream under the blazing road.

Koa

My mouth sores stink like slimy-skinned hīnālea rotting in the ipu kai.
Beloveds are ōhiʻa ʻai outside my screen door.

I peel enough bark from lower trunks to cover my hand.
A flush of brackish water and kukui soothes my appetite for unripe fruits.
I lure ʻōpelu with the kalo they like.

Beloveds are handsome cocks that jut from a wet understory's pulu.
Mahalo Kona sun—you warm my bathing place.

Rats gnaw the navel strings of aliʻi who steal my ʻōhiʻa ʻai.
Tsā! Let their teeth loosen while I muffle brother during kapu of silence.

My sores stink like crushed maile pilau.
No need kō to sweeten medicines for this angry mouth.

Brother with lucky earlobes and a head that wrecks canoes protects my screen door.
I chew my ʻōhiʻa ʻai while stomping royal shadows.
I approach flaming backs with machete, then simmer heads in vinegar and salt.

Mahalo Kona sun—you perch on my mind.
I'm ʻono for kalo flesh the color of wave breaks.
Kalo for choice kūlolo that eases my throat after a cleansing vomit.

Bitters

Jin cruises a reef where police throw nets and kāne eroded from smoke hide in the toilet to ask 'you get pipe?'
An 'awa-loosened kāne seeks lomi with anyone who will meet his gaze.
A kāne undercover bottoms up until his badge number tumbles out.
Aikāne bury an overindulgent hunter in a wild place for sprouting a potent sun-loving 'awa.

Jin laments until 'ono for eel and wet moans at the morning glory.
Ku'u Babe finds him restoring his 'umeke, then works the 'ōkolemakili with stone techniques.
They do right like Cadinot's tantric kāne pushing in juniorate, pressing in chalet.

Ku'u Babe checks his 100 sun-darkened walnuts and notices pronto 3 missing.
He grabs crickets relaxing on his cascara bag, spills some amber hue from a coupe etched FKB.
He stirs Jin's spirit base through synchronized breathing and multiple swells without rest.

Pua Kalikimaka

I weakened my stems so Big Matt would break them after we locked and 'o'o'ō!
as the victorious cock.
I played the Talking Book, but he didn't believe the music was Iesū's.
The disco Silvertone lit our faces yellow, pink, blue like bon odori lanterns
at our Temple of Great Happiness.

Mahalo Ke Akua for electricity.

My mother put a Kona Bottling Works crate near the stove so I could reach controls
while she explored night perfumed with gardenia or ylang ylang.
King's coil lifted my prayers through the Christ thorn we carried from Hōnaunau.

Big Matt scratched his pox until he looked like noni.
I said his beauty would be smooth again like a double-gourd drum, but he didn't care.

I wiped his sap after he gathered pua kalikimaka for placing at the Talking Book.
We reclined in our healing soda, heard the kerosene tongue burn pau pau pau.

Hāmākua barrack men tried wooing my mother with dead gamecocks.
Their playbooks didn't include removing bloody feathers first, so she never gave them chance.

During a moon bright enough to make shadows, I watched Big Matt steal lemons from a tree
of restless spirits.
He never snitched when his mother beat him.
I salved his acid blisters that swelled like distressed kōkala until I was afraid to touch.
I gave him my drawing called Kerosene Fairies and Night Chicken.

We stole daylight gardenias at Lanakila while my mother blew the head wounds of an auntie
who was pushed from a speeding Nova.
We cased a momiji grove of good red retention, pleasured on stolen loquat.
I angered Big Matt when I sought the secret knowledge poolhall boys shared in the forbidden
launderette, but I only found butane and wet socks sprouting birdseeds.

Mahalo Ke Akua for the boy spitting ola into his bruised father on their demon way to hell.

I missed Rock Bottom's sweet stink lua, the three-seated serenity of Hōnaunau's lua.
Ki'o in avocado shade and wiping with cool leaves offered new perceptions.

My mother sat us away from the udonya's bachi booth where an acquaintance killed a hired
hit squad, then disappeared up Mauna Loa.
I ate slippery food for easing wrong sleep.
Big Matt couldn't remember his dreams, so I turned his footboard west.

We watched the forest burn when the crematorium caught fire.
The smeared ash on his skin made me 'ono for aku.
I dreamed a speckled chicken led us through hau tangles into pō.
I woke with a sore lip.

A cousin we called Quarter-portion did nothing when Big Matt and some poolhall boys
tied me to pua kalikimaka along the road.

I struggled enough to hide my excitement of their pig grunts and firebrand eyes, then meditated
so passersby wouldn't see.

Big Matt alone on his lanai watched me loosen during an hour of indistinct visions.

The next day, I told Quarter-portion if he closed his eyes, I would put andagi in his mouth.
It was sun-beaten dogshit.

I placed third in an art contest called Sight is Beautiful with a likeness of myself tied
to pua kalikimaka.
My mother spent my cash prize on Benson & Hedges and gas from a merchant who she helped
launder money he kept in a cooler.

Policemen toppled my library, creased my town shirts, but found less than anticipated.
My mother said the interrogation became good cop, bad cop—so predictable.
When they slammed her against a wall and demanded names of suppliers, she asked
which one's Starsky, which one's Hutch?
She wrapped the jailhouse sandwich to go.

During a moon for successful planting, I gave Big Matt a cutting from the jade
my mother carried across ahupua'a.
He said he couldn't make the jade grow, so we planted it under a junkyard sign that warned
'Electrafid Fence.'

In my new village, a boy called Lonnie showed me suitcases of coke, cash bundles,
and pornography.
He played tapes of women asserting 'I don't like a long lick, I don't like a long dick,'
then lit a bullet that struck his na'au.
We called his foreskin a pizzer wizzer like a flame tree's bud.
He peeped through bedroom louvers to shout—you horny devils!

His father Harold told my mother he knew of her tight-lipped reputation.
Uncle fell naked from mango trees, hid in rubbish heaps with a spray bottle
for ambushing demons.
He answered his door once with only cowboy boots while women giggled on his loveseat.
My mother looked at his erection and said 'uh' 'is that what the fuss is about?' and told me
he was no longer able.

He taught me Sicilian defense for dangerous games, showed me Cab Calloway
hee dee hee dee hee dee hee at Kona Theater as it labored for breath.

Lonnie and I infiltrated luncheons off Aliʻi Drive with his mother Ivy who drove so close
to the edge on the road of the gods I could see passenger-side tires sending stones over the cliff.
When waves at Nāpoʻopoʻo were pau undoing auntie's top, we explored a mountain village
where souls depart.
I fed Chicago Mary lamb pulp after her amputations.
Her teeth rot made me hold breath.
I dialed Dirty Darnell's House of Wonders that welcomed heathen desires,
but the connecting kāne must have been fed too much crevice-loving hilu in the womb.
The Hard Love Club promised double fantasies but delivered spent ʻawa.
Auntie Ivy taught me the word emphysema.

We sought the palila's satisfaction upslurs.
Calls about mouflons and the coddling moth larvae.
Responses about the practiced palila knowing māmane of silky infestations.
They tell the story—their māmane, so plentiful before.

Auntie led us down Kaʻawaloa without water.

Not even the sheltering kou where I beat kapa alone could keep us from burning.

Auntie said she knew healer man Zoc's hut, then led us through foot-stabbing kiawe,

but I had only seen healer man walking the highway alone.

I wondered if the yellow queen in the sea glitter would lead nenue into net, into ʻumeke kou

of entrails and ʻinamona.

I invoked my kumu whose moonlight ʻōlelo kept my footwork smart.

A kumu who taught me to cross Kaʻohe's shifting stones without protection.

We had shared kūlolo when shadows weren't visible.

I ate from where kumu's spoon touched.

Though healer man Zoc kept vessels in shade, his water lit my throat

as I drank from where his lips touched.

Lonnie pressed play for jaguar love and other prophecies.

He mounted girls in pigshit grass, tried crashing us into Manago's after Auntie Ivy canceled pork night.

Through dusk my mother kept rice warm, and a door unlocked for Lonnie to sleep full.

I found her stolen pulu under his mattress.

'Ulu

Ānuenue

Tūtū kept
her ke'a in stone fissures
and stacked turtle shells after free eating

'Io who knew tūtū
love the air so wela

Tūtū stroked
the dark phases when 'io revealed
bathing pits in the kiawe

Tūtū stuck
thumb in my mother's piko
and saw 'oh . . . a boy' before my mother knew

Querents who listened tūtū
love the season so wela

She helped
junkies discern
the journey is no exile

A remembrance of bones placed
and octopus heads massaged into handsome shapes

Kiawe

The first time I walked away from Iesū was toward frilled muʻumuʻu and backstrap heels
the congregation never like boys wear because māhū are at the core of Satan's way.

I misted my pulses with the powder-sweet haikina Grandma Virgie gave me during a Low Sunday
lūʻau, then traveled north to Kailua town bathing in the haze of an ʻOle moon.

Auntie Patrice welcomed 'hey ho!' and showed my mother glamour shots from Honolulu.
Auntie opened her hale to teach Noble Truths she said would give me whatever I wanted.
I asked if anyone could walk The Middle Way in style like Sylvester's.
She said 'yeah, can,' unrolled sweet mats, then spread the brush clusters that satisfy
hungry ʻapapane.

While we lashed the ashy bark for lei, I heard the future call of a pū-blowing kāne.
The video bodhisattva looked like the reverend who said dung-eating māhū stay opposite
Ke Akua's purpose.

I asked if the butsudan auntie gave me in her town of good anchorage would make money come.
Auntie said 'going come.'

On the drive south, my mother said she couldn't believe auntie would spotlight
those Honolulu shots—so tacky.
I thought auntie looked like Jane Russell, real outlaw kine.
But my mother said even through the sepia, auntie's stretch marks were purple.
When she crushed a mongoose at Keauhou junction, the lazuli bracelet her ipo broke
came undone at the repair.

I placed carnation, flax, and tangerine in the esteemed loke lau's heart notes.
I chanted namu myōhō renge kyō until a peeping uncle accused me of demon worshipping.
He threw my backstraps over Kainaliu's cliff.

I asked my mother if The Middle Way led to scoffers of Ke Akua's fragrant sacrifice.
She didn't know.
She asked if I thought Auntie Patrice was leading us to fellowship.
I didn't know.

During climactic conditions, I found Iesū up a suckering kiawe that hung
with pod sugar and flowers.
Iesū called me so close I could see under his malo in the 'Ole moon's fast light.

I asked Iesū—can I abide in you while cruising unharmed over kiawe's thorns?
He said I changed up and strutted in dark that would overcome me.

I asked—can I abide under the half-leaf bats who survive on attacks from the rear?
He said gropers in dark ought to walk like him, away from crude teasing.

Iesū was over me at Hōnaunau's rodeo where shy 'ōpe'ape'a birth twins upside down.
Hōnaunau where enchanters with maka uliuli seek their own company.

Kahuna Man

Kahuna man blessed the Hōkūle'a and taught boys the 'ai kapu.
He told my father no need bathe as much as women—only they get the stink between their legs.

A village boy idled at our stone wall where Peter Moon serenaded Tūtū Clara his understanding
of drowsy Waipi'o.
Kahuna man kept his eyes covered where moths pollinate for heady events.
While my father dressed for holoholo in town, my mother stared at kahuna man from the shack
and chanted in her mind—look at me, I know you hear me, look at me you fucker.
Kahuna man removed his shades and pursed his lips into what my mother called
the butthole smile.

My mother shot vodka with Kumu hula Luahine in a Hōnaunau hut.
Wind swirled excelsior through wild growth of mīkana wahine.
Kumu's plunges and glides under rounding moons stimulated seeds and intuition.

If kumu spocked village girls cruising warships, kissing swabs, she heaved the haoles
into the rubbish.
Kumu left many kāhuna love calls unanswered.

I was birthed during an earthquake.
My mother mistook falling equipment and shattered glass as effects of the joint a nurse lit
in a supply closet.
I was named after a surfer who gave my mother his pāwale headdress.
His silver bowls kept ice melt from thinning kāmano lomi.
My mother passed him a joint and stories of natal waters that shine like new armor
after kāmano die.

Kahuna man came when my naʻau hardened and my cries threatened to level the shack.
He scolded my parents for stealing a Miloliʻi name, then wrote two new ones
on a seascape orientation.
He instructed my parents to choose, catch aʻama for offering, touch my forehead during sunrise,
remove the old name.
My true calling echoed a sound my mother wanted for life, so she was satisfied.

Five years after we moved up Kaʻawaloa, kahuna man and his intimate brought night business.
My mother hid our brushes and blocked me from kahuna man's face, but his kerosene shadow
traveled the house.

I dreamed body snatchers fanning sulfur, chewing rotten mū.
They let weevils of reclined hair eat my pith.
I screamed when burrowers hatched long belly segments in my ear.

I heard my mother kick kahuna man and his intimate back into the dark.
Hemū!

Buss Up Shut

Salisha teaches Kuʻu Babe buss up shut and goat night techniques.
Salisha tells Jin about her brokering days as The Bulldog of Des Moines.
They model elastic band jewelries, then catch Raja's tearful plea that his love-reluctant foreigner fulfill her promise.

In the den of the mountain fox, Salisha engages men talking business schemes,
but they question her expertise.
She asks if they have stock in waste management.
She says get some, then revisits the fox known for stealing money and serving low-reach spirits in flexible cups.

Jin asks about kerosene nights in Trinidad, but Salisha claims no memory.
Kuʻu Babe read that haoles were hacked in their gated villas along Trinidad's shore.
Salisha says things happen.
She produces beauty dish photos of her wā uʻi in pink bikini, an Aquarian kāne delighting eyes with his hulu and proportions.

While Kuʻu Babe works the tawa, Salisha says can you believe I married the man
who brought the Muslim girl a hotdog on a first date?

He took her on as secretary.
She typed his memos, he sought fixes for the misprints.
She typed more memos, he sought fixes again.
Her kāne delivered her reclined likeness from the uncommon realm of sculptors to her Leo fire
that attracts fans in loges and wine parlors.
Her kāne catches thrills when loaded moons agitate her poise.

Kuʻu Babe overhears her moʻopuna ask playmates for reasons anyone would name their kid
Kuʻu Babe.
After Salisha's boys eat the goat some guests left on their plates, Salisha sings a lullaby about babies
of foreign soldiers.
She remembers burning her arm on a kerosene lamp before electricity and shows Jin the memory
of her wound.

Kulu

At my house, I cleaned the lipstick sincerities my mother left Paniolo Cruz
and gave him a telephone message while he was legs to sea, fondling his hearing aid with one hand,
his ule with the other.
At his house, I followed bread recipes his deceased wife Estelle left in a basket,
washed monogrammed linens, and read her notes I found in the guestroom.

      Vivian put radish in the oxtail.
      Was oily and 'ono.

      I took pills by noon, but my legs don't always listen and the work punished my back.
      I need more napkins.
      I'm in the lua too much.

      Antennille sent Kaleo a card, so I reimbursed the twenty.
      Someone stole kapa from his trunk.
      Prescription ready pau hana.

I dreamed I was on a mean ocean and when I opened my eyes I was still dreaming
because the bulb burned out.
I hit my head in the dark.

Cesario's memory is dimming from the syphilis, but he manage.

Paniolo's grandson Adao became a secret companion of horses.
He rode them naked in rains that pleasure feathery jacarandas.
We lost ourselves in fleshy herbs.
He broke my zipper under a warm chimneypiece, pointed a rifle at me and said
show with your fingers how you lick pussy.

I read Estelle's notes while spinning her Patsy Cline records on a mid-century Zenith
until a flipped Chrysler burned the little grass shack after midnight.

Marlyn sorry she couldn't tell me about the ignition and invite us for Mass
because no one answered the door, but her kitchen always lepo.
We prayed for the executed man.

The hot water sounds like a siren and the rice button is stuck just like your doodoo
if you keep eating the jam.
Your utot is loud.

I let Josie use the saddle and gun.
She going rubbish the cans because they might catch fire.
Don't tell her I fell again.

To save the district from being overwhelmed, I rubbished the perfume Meleana bought
at the airport.
She caught Flavio holding a pillow on his cousin's face and when you try talk to him
he makes like a mongoose.
Don't worry I won't give them money.

I need the pot with the melted handle.

My mother called Paniolo Cruz a man of the wild ʻāina—he could shoe his own horse
and ride all night.
But she caught him investigating her sincerities through bedroom louvers.
The last time I saw Adao alive, we roughed under the double-blooming hibiscus
good for relaxing bowels.

The pierced boy of Kona Inn who sold divination tools became older brother when he showed me
his boyfriend stretching dough in a portrait miniature.
Older brother spocked me posing with imitation wisteria at Pay ʻn Save.
He called my shepherd hook ankh 'courage,' but I averted eyes and said
George Michael made me do it.

Joel developed images of nihonjin newlyweds, haoles climbing cajeput, all exposing themselves
like they were mourning.
After Hāliʻi of the blazing ʻehu left film, he and Joel fooled tourists with flashbulbs
while storytelling about kahiko night's kāne caught rocking chairs at Kamakahonu.

Hāliʻi showed me photos of his kāne in a memory book organized by district.
I saw Adao loving a brindled dog under an ʻohe that began sleeping for hot months.
I pretended not to know him.

When I said Hāliʻi requested my image and kissed my ankh a hui hou, older brother gave me
a protection spell.
I prayed with wet hair and dreamed centipedes enjoying longevity.

The first time my mother photographed Tūtū Clara, she passed a finger at the lens.
The developed image was a night of swelling ipu.

Joel and I went holoholo roadster to Laʻaloa's vanishing sands for kissing in the ulu niu—
oh boy boy and how.
Blue-eyed baby handled my elastic, then told me a neighbor molested him in a locked cottage.
He convinced a curious sister they were only rehearsing by tying a bow around Joel's neck.
I said sorry Joel, but he said no need because he liked it.

I told how brothers Remy and Dwight painted their fox faces indigo to hide loot
in Kona Theater's splintered wings.
Their father wounded them during a mad sleepwalk.
Remy tore my book of animal worship, then overpowered me for Dwight to lower my corduroys
and say 'don't worry, we're like that.'
Dwight shaved himself bald after starting a mohawk in the wrong spot.
Remy tried murder-suicide with a gas stove.

Hāli'i and I went holoholo jeep into Hualālai's rainshadow where he glowed like conceiving heat.
He massaged stories out my spine in the ease of his koali swing.
I told about Lincoln who left Jamaica for raising David in L.A., then left a starlet
and Paul Newman's soirées for tending 'uala and weed.
Lincoln clapped louder than the bulb-loving roaches when David spun me in mu'umu'u.
We made weapons in the bamboo forest.

Lincoln fed kids of the red dust uncooked eyes and divined smoke from burning rubbish.
After a sweat-stained haole called us mongrels at a Hilo gas line, I dreamed we cooked her
crooked shape into a low suds soap for scrubbing pōpoki's box.
My mother showed nudies of ketchup covered women reclined on giant hamburger buns
that gave me nightmares.

I chased my mother chasing Lincoln across ʻaʻā, she wielded his cornmeal cake apology like a shot.
We ate it without him and listened for changing currents.
She kept Lincoln's dreadlock in a lacquered box.

Hāliʻi revealed buds of kokiʻo ʻulaʻula, said he would entice my spirit into a big toe
by making the hōkiokio whistle Portuguese Love.
He would drape maile kaluhea on my body and catch my fluttering spirit with his hōkeo
if I shared water from mine.
He would massage the legs, the breast, the throat.
A first cock to ʻoʻoʻō!

I dreamed the nanana hatched young under my leaves.
Her abdomen mask vanished during night hunts.
Practitioners cut blooms from my body, then backed away in gratitude.
I heard fevered patients moan as practitioners scattered my dust over running sores.
When I woke, my piercing was infected.

I stitched a silver J on my collar before exploring a verdant situation where ʻelepaio heard Joel say
he will marry a woman to please his parents and their money.
ʻElepaio watched us catch zenith stars in a dirty sock.
ʻElepaio pecked at trunks unworthy of the adze.

I followed Hāliʻi's call through guava shade like a desirous ʻapowai.
He was stripping his maile in leaping waters that coaxed the maiʻa to unsheathe.
I obeyed the dawn opening in the muddy pool.
I saw a nose-down dog reflected until the leaky moon made me forget to test the water with lau kī.

Make Man Sleep

I crawl from the rotted stump to moan with a red-throated kāne
'ō—thrust
'ō—now pivot
'ō

We burn the kāwelu on worn basalt
Dog eaters make love grasses tremble
We burn the wind twisted kāwelu of unprotected slopes

After fascinated eyes find him on the promenade
my telephone bills bloat like a courting 'iwa

He stabs when I like holoholo
He says no kāne wants a deformed gourd

I sprinkle crushed 'ōlena and kai
for make man dreams of kāwelu tolerating drought

I crawl from the sun's excrement to help jocks huli numbers
and interpret clouds above leeward center

They say my talk is māhū talk
and slap it from my mouth

They tear my kūpe'e then laugh
as I mend the palai that repels little intruders

Before I make man with open mouth to let my talk return
I pray over palai that treats madness
Amen over sharp kala whose mouths are open too

Caretakers surround my corpse while doctor with skin like a salmon's ass
comes when he comes and shouts so every mourner can hear—
why hurry me
he's not going anywhere

Before I leap into the versina
I tell salmon ass—
in the din over your corpse
mourners will smash their teeth and expose so there's no mistaking their grief

I climb the mooring holes at Ka Lae to visit sister-of-the-decoy-basket
Our stained hooks tell us where fishes multiply

I ready her scalp tonic of sprawling ʻākala
but she won't let me touch
I wash my own ʻumeke in a brackish pit

Sister savors amaro
speculates why tūtū loosened gods for my birth

Sister scratches kāki'o then wipes hands on my bed
seeks my hair and other bait

If I return, I may offer speckled eggs to the caldera's fire
I might sleep make man head to sea for more instruction

Robby

Tūtū of dogs who group for battle knelt with me at Kahikolu.
After her niece covered the coke when I saw her snorting off our good Formica,
my mother said no hide em—better he understands the true condition.
Her ipo thought māhū belonged destitute.
I prayed Ke Akua would keep CPS from returning.

Tūtū sewed culottes for Kona's cheerleaders who knew modesty
unlike north side titas of reddish water.
Tūtū said Kona's daughters will not flash ass on any field like east side titas of the upright cliff.

Football boys charged the banner I scented with Waiʻaleʻale's leathery berries.
I painted concentrics and Robby's urge number in gold-brown like his skin with a hala fruit brush.
Reservoirs rumbled in the core.
Then came the plunge pool level where keen listeners offer the larvae of energetic fliers.
Above, olomea sticks ignited the softer hau.
More above, contagious magic kept Robby alert when the sky was red like noni root dye.

I did the funky chicken for Robby whose smooth, coconut oiled body attracted kāhuna looking to carve bones into supernatural hooks.
Tūtū said some boys shake caboose in culottes, but I knew was wicked.

My father pried my door so he and three strangers could conspire before traveling every district to trade safety for kālā.
He gave me a birthday shirt with pink script 'Girl Watcher' under a Nia Peeples lookalike.
While I tested the shirt on Māmalahoa, surly-eyed Solomon threw stones from an arsenic bush that was turning from light to die.

Pak!
Māhū!
Pak!
You get Vaseline fo take em up da ass?
Pak!

I called the talkative stranger The Deutschland Devil because his namesake was a bel canto seer who pleaded with moonlit chicken feathers.

I showed the Devil my shrine of Wil Wheaton posing L.A. finery, his signature in gold metallic.

When the Devil requested vinegar for Deutschland stew, my mother gave Auntie Bea directions by pointing lips.

Auntie crept from the toilet, then conjured a bottle of mother fungus.

She led Stranger René's yen for instant romance to the 'awapuhi rustle.

Auntie slept late.

Between the rift zone and Pāhala's red-yellow ash, I told Zazen Stranger about a haole of the coarse mat.

The haole broke a woman's skull while his 'partner in crime' they pronounced 'pic' captured it on VHS.

Experts diagnosed 'pathological drunk,' so cops gave him IZ-wide boroz, then kicked him from the clink.

The haole was seen sticking one thumb on the belt highway, the other in a belt loop to keep the boroz up.

The revived woman burned his house with VHS kindling and never saw the ʻōhiʻa lehua
budding through scorch.

Where the blind moʻo ate thirsty men, Uncle Sunny paid ten bucks for my piss in a Ziploc
so he could work the sugar mill.
Where dunes vanished pools for wāhine bathing, I told Zazen Stranger
my mother pulled me from school, then gave a rundown over loco moco diminished
by McCormick chicken.
She said two nihonjin in splendid attire sought Uncle Sunny but never mentioned
a most likely theft.
The one with a missing pinky chuckled when she asked if they were going to shorten her fingers.

After trading safety for kālā in the cleansing Kanilehua, the leeward hui treated me
Prince Kūhiō Plaza—magazines promised Menudo's sizzling centerfold, Tom is a lonely Top,
George and Andrew pack a double.
My father bought the 'I love pōpoki' acrylic with pink puff vinyl I coveted for Mamu's image.
The hui squared biz at Reflections where I watched myself eat dorado, the acrobatic strugglers.

Cheetah-kāne seized my candy-striped cowry to overcome pressure induced by the load.
He let me stretch his nylon malo, then told me the umbra excitement of his wā liʻiliʻi's eclipse
made him bite another boy's lip.
I told him the Trueloves died on the deuxième two nights apart and the doctors kept calling them
Lovejoys by mistake.

On the first night of the wahine's passing, my nostrils stretched in a dream of chewing astringent
hala with silver teeth.
I soaked my sheets on the second night of the kāne's passing when a kahuna countered
a shit-eating death dealer whose bitter fish hooked my soul.
The kahuna returned it with a worn horse's naʻau and a ti leaf broom.
I woke ʻono for hāwane, so I climbed the loulu trunk notched over one hundred years.

After silencing Mrs. Endo's heart bleep machine, my kolo kolo kolo! aroused cheetah-kāne
from medicated sleep.
His groin smelled like oily maruya.

I said when Mrs. Endo hired me to weed peonies and coxcombs, I razed everything in an act of unintentional evil until her terrace looked like Puna's denuded fish basket.

Mr. Endo bought us a Tercel I cruised through remote places draped with devil's ivy.
I found kāne riding thighs on plastic adirondack.
Mr. Endo gave me Ajax, crisp twenties and katsu at the model house I scoured until its silver stopped reflecting.

On the model bed, I dreamed the receiver who captivates with the forepart that puckers like an eel's mouth.
I never touched the wet instrument I used to praise Robby in my sleep, but I confessed anyway.

While Hilo was dreaming in adze-sculpted minds, I watched Mr. Endo spending money and my mother wasting time at Reflections.

For the first three days of the new year, I ate Mrs. Endo's kuri kinton that treats delirious speech.
Mrs. Endo filled my mouth with nihamaguri I spit into her toilet.

If she answered after my mother dialed Mr. Endo, my mother said hūi manang es tu?
Hūi manang!
Click.

In my hatsuyume, my mother asked if we should blackmail Mr. Endo.
I extended breath uuuuuuuuuuuuu to keep the sun from setting.
Mrs. Endo went Vegas and won big.

I's the cave-hiding coward with pōpoki whose little heart beat so fast and a monthly that promised
first love intimacies on page 36.
I's the sleeping pills swallower left to flex and rot on the open mound.
In the final calm, Robby repaired mesh entrance the size of three fingers.
I ripened fish viscera, wove his malo on my backstrap loom.
We fed a long-headed pig cold uhi and dog food.
We swam the pig at Hōnaunau's reef where the wana no villager deifies
attracts round-snouted eels.

Robby strangled the pig, then carved the bone shafts while I pounded 'ulu into a mass
of three hand lengths.
I could fist from an outstretched arm.
Cocked ears knew the waiting was over in our home of double descent.
My rhythm was the lifetimes I traveled for Robby to be with me blowing my mind.

But my best tita revived me so we could holoholo in the pohā forest where boys hydraulic pump.

When the sail hung limp, I showed cheetah-kāne wahine Truelove's newspaper mahalo
for the corrective lenses a neighbor gifted.
I cleaned kāne Truelove, then wrapped him like a long fish.
Nurse Marisol lightened her skin with calamansi oil and showed me a purse of gems,
a green Mercedes, other possessions her congregant titas envied.

I heard crying from the man who was just told the HIV made his resistance pau.
Nurse Marisol tut-tutted, 'that's what he gets for screwing around.'

I didn't know how to comfort him without being seen, so I called in my mind—you were born snake radiant, you dream wā uʻi dreams in a room number of fire.
The fire that singes pig bristles.
Warmth your beloveds wear as garments.

Robby and I fished with human poles where we could see each other in the light of first calm.
We protected ʻuala plots from mountain pig raids.

During a threat of fountaingrass fire, we dressed a temporary hut with purple yam flowers, then went Hualālai for the uhiuhi that purifies blood.

Pō

Mahalo kūmū of the ancient hole.

Salt-rolling winds stimulate our flows near breathing pots and objects for lovemaking.
Salt gathers at north entrances for protecting our funk.
We illuminate moth killing grounds where blind mortises hide their girths.

Mahalo kūmū of blood color.

When a mat of elegant weft is ready, ipo strokes on the sweet hīnano while moʻo prophets spit
into my mouth and assure—no animal has crossed the salt basket.

We consume the handsome kūmū and juice from slanting ulehala's nourishing tips.
Naʻauao mākou.

Kukui

I lifted leg on the belt highway like Claudette with roller skates and knife.
A gracious stranger drove me and my 'ulu to north Kona's broiling pits
where hoaloha Bizu was killed.
I fed Bizu's spirit the broiled flesh, said I was going Puna to woo.
He muttered 'you lucky bastard.'
I left Kona with silver buttons the stranger tore from his shirt.

My shimmering greasepaint made some vigorous kāne of Kohala wink.
The Moaʻe kū blew my hair into a Meliʻsa Morgan kine style for captivating their minds.
I serviced Kohala's prepared kāne who knew the ways of pelvic heat.
They gave me fragrant lei and sugar cane that can wound the mouth.

Some folks on Honokaʻa's drag avoided my roller skates by taking long corners.
I left with land shells that enamor in dappled light.

I met another māhū in Honomū on their way to bury milk teeth somewhere near Māwae.
They had lashes like pandanus thorns.
They said Puna's abundance is choice for cock-fetching in a fine climate.

I performed the puppet hula of damselflies grooming in Kapoho.
Damselflies locking for the heart-shape mating pulse.
I made strong kāne in Kapoho slope back.

The one whose trunk I toppled on the foreshore took me Ka'ū.
We chopped the mitts of loose characters down with o.p.p.
We made long Ka'ū beautiful from end to end.
We aged in kukui groves, then sank into the earth.

Kona of yearning māhū bows to handsome Kohala, to Hāmākua of landslides and the long mound.
Hilo, famous for the curative sea of Mokuola.
And who can forget Ka'ū that reclines for Puna, Puna that reclines for Ka'ū?

Pipipi

The māmā runs ahahana across wet jags
and spits pipipi into boy's mouth

The māmā plucks winter grays from her body
then dresses boy for running ehehene

While boy's skull is soft
the māmā massages mudflat tactics
into boy's jaw for snatching 'a'ama

The māmā tells about whispering sky migrants
in the green shelled universe

After boy's flight muscles strengthen enough
to search cliffsides that hide bones and feathers
boy catches the oversummered māmā's final
hā

in a length of bamboo
then wades through lua dark with salt-loving kīpūkai
the color of the māmā's feet

Made in the USA
Columbia, SC
13 May 2024

35100549R00087